Contents

EARTHQUAKE!

Written by Dot Meharry
Illustrated by Sandra Cammell

Hippopotamus went to sleep.

3

Along came Monkey.

"Here is a rock to sit on," said Monkey.

She climbed up.

5

"*Humph!*" said Hippopotamus.

8

Hippopotamus woke up.
"Was there an earthquake?"
she said.

Match

Match each animal to the letter it begins with.

12

VULTURE VISIT

Fun Fact

A vulture's bald head is easy to keep clean.

Did You Know?

A vulture eats animals that are already dead.

11

VERA THE VULTURE

"I'll never eat veggies,"
vowed Vera the Vulture.
So Vera got leaner
and leaner.
Until, very early
one Valentine's Day,
she vanished up
the vacuum cleaner.

Them Up

Match each capital letter to its small letter.

GETTING FOOD

Written by Dot Meharry

A butterfly has a long tongue.

A frog has a long tongue.

17

A snake has a long tongue.

An anteater has a long tongue.

18

A giraffe has a long tongue.

A long tongue helps some animals get food.

19

21

ZOO

The Map at the Zoo

N
W   E
S

Written by Dot Meharry
Illustrated by Annabel Craighead

Path   Picnic Area   Lake

22

Key

Alligators

Bears

Birds

Camels

Elephants

Giraffes

Hippos

Lions

Meerkats

Monkeys

Pandas

Tigers

Zebras

Dad and I went to the zoo.
"Where are the lions?" I said.

Dad looked at the map.
"The lions are this way," he said.
"Come on!"

We went...

past the meerkats...

past the elephants...

and past
the monkeys.

"There are no lions here!" said Dad.

I looked at the map.
"Come on," I said.
"The lions are this way."

We went...

past the giraffes...

past the zebras...

and past
the hippos
to the...

31

lions!

"You had the map
upside down, Dad!" I said.

33

Three Little Monkeys

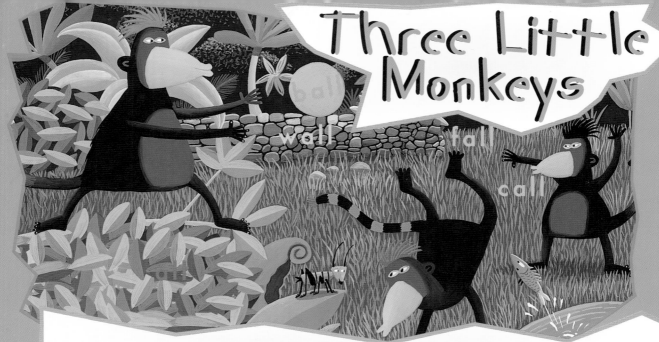

Three little monkeys play with a ball.

Three little monkeys shout and call.

Three little monkeys
play on a wall.

Three little monkeys
take a fall.

Letters I Know

 **Ll**  **Vv**  **Zz**

Sounds I Know

-all

Words I Know

along	here	said
are	long	shouted
came	looked	this
has	past	went